This Wine Into Water

This Wine into Water

edited
by
Lorna Crozier

Wintergreen Studios Press
Township of South Frontenac
PO Box 75, Yarker, ON, Canada K0K 3N0

Copyright © 2018, with copyright retained by individual authors. All rights reserved under the International and Pan-American Copyright Conventions. No part of this book may be reproduced in any form or by electronic or mechanical means, including information storage and retrieval systems, without permission in writing from the publisher, except by a reviewer, who may quote brief passages in a review. The views expressed in this work are those of the authors and do not necessarily reflect those of the publisher. Wintergreen Studios Press (WSP) gratefully acknowledges financial support from Wintergreen Studios.

Book and cover design by Rena Upitis
Edited by Lorna Crozier with Susan Alexander & Susan Wismer
Cover watercolour by Melanie Craig-Hansford

Composed in Book Antiqua and Candara, typefaces designed by Monotype Typography and Gary Munch, respectively.

Library and Archives Canada Cataloguing in Publication
Crozier, Lorna.
This Wine Into Water/Lorna Crozier
ISBN: **978-1-989321-00-3**
Poetry — General.
I. Title. This Wine Into Water.
Legal Deposit — Library and Archives Canada

Wintergreen Chapbooks

Momma's Prayer Flags (2015)

Sound Me When I'm Done (2016)

Teasing the Tongue (2017)

Contents

Daily Miracles 1

Argument 4

Food for Thought 6

This Body 8

The Sound of Sadness 9

Bears 10

Ashes 11

Journey 12

Everyone's Gone to Bed 13

A Suicide Note 14

Humpty's Version 15

A Sound of Sadness, A Sound of Joy 17

Silence: Questions and Answers 18

Familiarity 19

Rose-Red 20

A Photographer Goes to the Nursing Home 22

Wintergreen Pond, Early Morning 23

Morning Mist 24

Kerosene Lamp and Candlelight 25

Contributors 27

Daily Miracles

Turning this wine into water. We know the allusion—the original story from the Gospel of John: Jesus at the Marriage of Cana doing the opposite of what this title claims. Water into wine was his first miracle, at least the first recorded. You might ask, why does it come up here, in reverse, as a title for a chapbook of poetry written at Wintergeen?

Katie Thompson, a poet who is always questioning, always lifting corners of darkness in the sleeping house, gave us the idea. She writes with such bravery and humour: *God? Have that son of yours turn this wine into water and I will walk upstairs and greet you in person.*

Ah, you must read the whole poem to discover why water is the holier of the two liquids in the world of her poem, but no matter what substance changes into what, Katie reminds us that poetry is the art of transformation. It turns the common twenty-six letters of the alphabet, ancient, dusty and often poorly used, into poems that challenge, delight and honour our short time on earth. Words themselves, I believe, become sacred when they are transformed into the blessing we call poetry.

Many poems we read come close to the sacred because of the writer's rapt attention, one that dusts the observed with a secular reverence. Suzanne Doerge achieves that in her reluctant paean to night where she walks us through the speaker's fear: "But by stepping outside my own circle of light, I stepped / into yours…Kerosene lamp and candlelight." Susan Alexander shows us a different kind of luminosity, one oral, olfactory, and tactile, in her erotic tribute to bees: "I could hear the bees hum / deep inside their cluster, smell / a trace of summer's / honey. I'd never felt so warm."

Susan Wismer suggests plentitude and awe in the final line of her summer pond haiku. We're used to Basho's single frog in the still pond, but at Wintergreen, Susan sees "Ten frogs jump." Her line says so much about the natural and creative fecundity of the place. And Ruth McKinney creates such sweet poignancy and loss in "…the kayak sitting in the tall grass / waiting for its owner to be young again." Of course, in the midst of the miraculous and sacred, there's room for humour. Julia McArthur's praise poem to bears makes them, not us, the superior species. "Exemplary bears," she says as she sums up her list of their ursine attributes.

Poetry's closeness to the miraculous comes partly from its marriage to music. Its vision, its argument, its logic cannot be separated from the half rhymes and cadences of the phrases held within the confines it imposes on itself. You can hear the images becoming song in Kathryn MacDonald's impeccable lines: "In the windless woods / a leaf falls with the grace of a mime," and in Melanie Craig-Hansford's question, "Have you ever felt your soul crumble / beneath the eyes of ghosts?"

In the opening line of the first entry in this collection, Callista Markotich's "Argument" reminds us that poetry's closest companion is silence: "We posit that there is no sound for sadness." In the act of composition, poets pull every single word out of an existential hush. Each choice implies dozens of nouns, adjectives and verbs abandoned, rejected, never said. Callista goes on to refute her opening by offering in leaps of imagination and exactitude how sadness might come to live in the ear.

Elizabeth Paulette-Coughlin shows us another oral equivalency of sadness in her touching description of "blue / larkspur on a tombstone / of a baby / whose soul / has passed over." And

Sandra Campbell in answer to her poem's question, "What makes silence painful?" shakes us to the core with her answer, "The silence after you ask: do you love me?" A silence that demands such an intense listening guides us into the presence of poetry's amplitude and grace. In the company of these eleven Wintergreen poets, we are drinking water, we are drinking wine.

Lorna Crozier
November 2018

CALLISTA MARKOTICH

Argument

We posit that there is no sound of sadness.
Let us suppose that somewhere on an evening this September

a husband drives home from his vigil at a hospice,
walks from the driveshed to the farmhouse back door,
kitchen empty but for trays and bowls from neighbour wives;

a young mother tiptoes up the stairs and creeps along
the hall to her bedroom — oh, to reach the door at the end,
where she will fall to sleep, or weep, all night;

a son sits rocking on the wide plank porch
of the family camp, the firepit cold, the cottage dark.
He stares at the glimmering lake.

> *a barn owl calls*
> *a child whispers "Mommy?"*
> *a loon hurls its clear cry into the night air*

But they hear nothing.
Body and soul, they brim with loss,
There isn't space for a decibel to enter.

There is no sound of sadness.
Let us suppose that somewhere on an evening in September, one year hence

a husband hears a barn owl's call. He finds it pleasing, fitting,
imagines wide wings sailing low over the stubbled field,
claiming dominion of the kingdom of tiny creatures there.

From the half open door in the upstairs hall, a young mother
hears her name whispered: "Mommy?"
She tiptoes in, hugs her daughter, fluffs a pillow, kisses a forehead.

A son hears a loon cry into the night air. He thinks it
evocative. He thinks how his father loved that sound.
He thinks he will paint their cottage next spring.

We posit that people are sad,
sounds are sounds.

CALLISTA MARKOTICH

Food for Thought

Raven, seeing far into the future, calls a council.
Elephant, seeing far into the past, comes early.
Wise and unselfish, he knows his bulk, his swaying gait
alarms the smaller beasts, especially Tick.
Sea Turtle, a quiet influence, a keen environmentalist,
though also ponderous, moves slowly, so that no one is risked.
Anyway, he arrives late, in ancient ritual that has served him well,
as Hare could tell you.
Raccoon, Waste Management and Food Distribution Chair, is to preside.
Tick is present for Climate Change, Deforestation, and Exotic Human Ailments.
Attendance is low, for many members think the group impotent.
God, the real chair, never comes.
Everything is tabled.

Raven speaks: Mr. Chair, change is coming in matters of food.
God will call down, in the nations of plenty, a plague called *allergy*.
He will call down a plague called *intolerance*. There will be almost nothing,
in the nations of plenty, that a human can eat. Food from the
ground will bear disease. Food from above the ground will be
tainted with substances inedible and dangerous.
There will be grave diseases amongst humans from foods they eat.
Yet they will grow fat.
And there will cover the earth and fill the seas of the nations of plenty,
everlasting waste called *plastic*. All will change.

Raccoon speaks: With respect sir, we will adapt. We always have.
Our numbers are many and our fingers nimble. We have already
mastered a new difficulty called *packaging*.

Raven speaks: No. God is angry about matters of food, in the
nations of plenty.

Elephant clears his mighty throat and speaks: God was angry once
and sent a flood.

Sea Turtle replies: I recall. But then God was young, impulsive.
Does he punish us again, as an old, tired god? For if it is so, we will
suffer without end. God must retire.
We must solve these problems ourselves.

Raven speaks: This idea has merit. You, Sea Turtle, must form a
delegation.
You must go to talk to God about this matter.
And so it was moved, seconded and passed. And to this day,
they await the answer, as Sea Turtle cannot be rushed,
any more than God.

They prepare to adjourn, and Elephant speaks, swinging his large
head, which still bears a magnificent set of ivory tusks:
Yet we still have the problem of humankind.

Tick speaks: Mm hmm.

ELIZABETH PAULETTE-COUGHLIN

This Body

this body is a body
that loves what it loves:
black velvet dresses,
oil of roses,
the piano of Satie.

at the edge of waterfalls
this body will take its time
before making the final
slide.

yet, when I dream of you
it is not this body
but something wild.

dark body, cloaked in feathers
i plunge towards you, warm,
and wet as your tongue.
dying to myself
in the art of body,
                        breathing.

ELIZABETH PAULETTE-COUGHLIN

The Sound of Sadness

The sound of sadness
is blue
larkspur on the tombstone
of a baby whose soul
has passed
over.

A small blue blanket.

I watched my mother lift
his tiny body
from a carriage
by the well.

Even the hemlocks
were silent.

JULIA MCARTHUR

Bears

Bears don't get the respect they deserve.
Can we hibernate for months,
Recycling our urine, so we don't poison ourselves?
Can we decide, nope, not enough calories to conceive right now,
Better wait awhile?
Impressive built-in family planning.
Amazing bears.

Enviable bears lose fat, not muscle mass in hibernation.
Can we do that?
What would you give
For that annual weight loss program?

Admirable bears eat locally and seasonally:
Grass, buds and new leaves in spring;
Berries, bugs, and small rodents in summer.
Rich acorns in the fall, nuts and seeds,
To fatten up by hibernation time.
How smart, to sleep through dark cold winter!
No dangerous migration to Florida or Mexico.
Exemplary bears.

KATHRYN MACDONALD

Ashes

In the windless woods
a leaf falls with the grace of a mime.
And in a ragged nest
the hollow bones of the red tail hawk
remember flight   the song of feathers.

Through the empty house stillness settles
coals in the woodstove a mere glow.

In the deep silence of night
your voice   vibrant with life
whispers my name.
I listen   search the dark
for the shape of you

touch your pillow   still smooth
and I remember.

KATHRYN MACDONALD

Journey

> "Leave the door open to the unknown…go."
> from *A Field Guide to Getting Lost* —Rebecca Solnit

Now summer has lost its steamy heat
the fragrance of clover   snow-buried.
In our room   the coverlet pulled up
my pillow plumped   the door open.

Adrift like a pilgrim
my back to what cannot be faced
   the absence of your face
   your body that pleasures me.

By day safaris distract
   zebras and elephants
      hippopotami in the river.   A lion pair
lying side-by-side in tall grass

haunt my sleep.   By night
I shut my eyes   to see
the curl of your hair   to feel
your lingering touch   the moisture between us.

KATIE THOMPSON

Everyone's Gone to Bed

And you, wandering the lights-out kitchen of the sister you love most. Poking around in the fridge, the liquor cabinet. Afraid to wake the sleeping house. Hush. Yourself.

A man at group, your age but beautiful, said there's a hole in his chest and the wind blows through. Someone else's line, but he's earned it.

The emptiness staggers. It's why we meet in church basements even while pretending the god doesn't apply. *God? Have that son of yours turn this wine into water and I will walk upstairs and greet you in person.*

MELANIE CRAIG-HANSFORD

A Suicide Note

Under the guise of promised matrimony
Hamlet came to my bed chamber.
One day they will call his crime rape.
One day, my fair maidens,
we will rise up and stop these crimes of the flesh.

Have you ever felt your soul crumble
beneath the eyes of ghosts?
My spirit is fallen like a dam
holding back the water that calls me home.
Let the flower that Hamlet has taken from me
      rest in my hair.
They say I was divided from myself
      and my fair judgment.
Judge me not for I have never seen so clearly.

I write this final letter,
this, the first decision I have made of my own free will.
My father dead, my brother preoccupied.
Let the pre-Raphaelites have their way with me
      in paint,
Let the song writers and story tellers immortalize me.
Let the willow branch upon which I rest
      break,
as Hamlet has broken me.

RUTH MCKINNEY

Humpty's Version

For Kylie and Max

My Mother was a silly Goose
She wrote a song, just four lines long
to say I fell.
Well, … she was wrong.

I didn't really fall…at all!

I jumped!!   Kerthumped!

And it wasn't really a wall…at all.

It was a fence!

On the fence too long
Same old song.
Thin or Fat?
Round or Flat?
Dog or Cat?

The nation divided.
I thought.
Decided.

Fat, Flat, Cat.
I jumped. Ker -

SPLAT!!!

Bad choices may not work, it seems
So here I lie in smithereens
And so dear children, there's the truth
As told you by your great-aunt, Ruth

I didn't really fall…at all!

RUTH MCKINNEY

A Sound of Sadness, A Sound of Joy

The sound of sadness is a sigh
from the kayak sitting in the tall grass
waiting for its owner to be young again.

A sound of joy is the shriek of laughter from the tiny
neighbour children running naked at dusk,
chasing the chickens their parents gave them so
they would know where eggs come from.

Silence: Questions and Answers

1. Question: What's silence?
   Answer: Absence of noise.

2. Question: Are you ever silent?
   Answer: Not yet, there's the breath: in out, in out.

3. Question: Are you too old to be afraid of silence?
   Answer: Still too young not to fear it.

4. Question: What makes a silence painful?
   Answer: The silence after you ask: do you love me?

SANDRA CAMPBELL

Familiarity

His banner over me was love.
In our early days I refused
its shelter—too unfamiliar,
reasoning confinement instead.
It took a while—for the familiarity,
I mean.

SUSAN ALEXANDER

Rose-Red

" ...and when he came up to them suddenly his bearskin fell off, and he stood there a handsome man, clothed all in gold. 'I am a king's son,' he said, 'and I was bewitched.'" from Grimm's Fairy Tales

I kept the pelt. It was the colour of my hair,
smelled clean as a rowan tree.
At last, alone. I wrestled
his bearskin from the chest in my stateroom,
buried my face in fur and remembered
my mother's cottage, winter nights
beside the hearth, toying
with that dark storm.

The wooden door shattered on broken
iron hinges. I loped through
the open gate, beyond the screams, swifter
than any pony, through bush and bramble as if
called to this clearing. Morning mist rose
and I too stretched up
higher, higher. My nails
tore through bark like knives
through butter, and I roared.

After that came snow and the quiet.
Hare, roe, stag, badger in its sett.
I could hear bees hum
deep inside their cluster, smell

a trace of summer's
honey. I'd never felt so warm.
Then, at last, came the long sleep.
In branching dreams, I search
for bilberries with their shine of wild jewels,
I watch my mother prune her roses.

SUSAN WISMER

A Photographer Goes to the Nursing Home

I. Hilda

It's my hands that I want.
I'll just put them here.
Go ahead.

II. Ruth

I like myself best from the back.
I think that I'd like to be looking away
at a tree, or a leaf, or a cloud in the sky.
Where? I don't know —
Just somewhere that says, please come.
You look too.

III. Barbara

Take that wooden chair. Put it under the tree.
I'm going to wear nothing
but this clean white sheet, best use
that it's had, I would say.
Drape me like this, we'll tuck it in there —
don't ask how I learned this, who I was —
It's who I am now they should see.

My face, the white sheet, my shoulders and arms,
the shadows, the sun on my face. That's what I want.

I want them to see me, looking at them,
proud and old.

There's beauty in that, don't you know.

SUSAN WISMER

Wintergreen Pond, Early Morning

Bare feet, cool green grass
One dew pearl shimmers —
Ten frogs jump

Morning Mist

morning mist on placid lake
ascends   subsides
        breath
                      shifts
new day's mystery floats
                across clear glass
hush drifts into unexplored spaces
        opens
              yields
silence folds into silence
        unfolds   folds afresh
awe rolls over to kiss the shores
              soft and slow
then stretches audacious toward the sky
enticing clouds to meet in the in-between
        expands
enchants
              blinds
once inside boundaries dissolve
this mist
        limitless
                      love

SUZANNE DOERGE

Kerosene Lamp and Candlelight

We were young women, in love in the city, when you announced
you were moving out, to a one room cabin, no electricity, alone
in the woods. Kerosene lamp and candlelight.

It cracked my heart, as we had schemed to do that together,
driving country roads, looking for just the right spot. It was your
way to say you could go it alone. Kerosene lamp and candlelight.
You were tired of being in my shadow.

It's taken me a while, nearly forty years, to face my fears of staying
here, alone, in an isolated cabin. Kerosene lamp and candlelight.
Troubling sounds in the night and echoes of women's screams
that somehow you kept away as if you had an invisible shield you
drew around your young self.

Now, as I lean forward to blow the last candle out, the silence
in these walls causes me pause. Surreptitious presence. I hear you
whisper from your side of the great divide, "*I've been with you all
along,*"
your head tilted to the side and smiling. *"I just wanted you to believe,
like I wanted too, that you can do what you fear the most."*

I have lived my own courageous acts. Kerosene lamp and candlelight. But stepping outside my own circle of light, I stepped into yours. Of course, it is here where we would reconvene. Kerosene lamp and candlelight.

Contributors

Callista Markotich is a retired Teacher, Principal and Superintendent of Education who is delighted to be writing poetry rather than memos and reports. She lives in Kingston, Ontario. Recent winner of *The 1000 Islands Playhouse* Canada-themed writing contest, her poems have also been selected for The *Nashwaak Review* and *Riddlefence*.

Elizabeth Paulette-Coughlin is a yoga teacher, therapeutic bodyworker and aspiring poet. She runs poetry circles in Montreal called Poetry as Prayer with the cellist, Iona Corber. Elizabeth has a special passion for her porch in the country overlooking Lake Memphramagog. It is here that she has learned the sacred ways of wind from her many different windchimes.

Julia McArthur lives and works in Kingston by the lake. At Wintergreen she is inspired by Lorna's teaching, Rena's energy, and the generous support of fellow poets.

Melanie Craig-Hansford is a poet, artist, soul searcher, tree hugger and animal lover (not necessarily in that order). She is grateful for Rena's vision, Wintergreen Studios, Lorna and Patrick's wisdom and generosity, and for all the poets who have gathered there over the years and shared their love of poetry.

Sandra Campbell writes fiction and non-fiction and has tried her hand at a few docs. She treasures her Wintergreen retreats with Lorna whose words and ways open her to the deep mystery of trying to express the ineffable in words.

Kathryn MacDonald is a writer living in Eastern Ontario. *A Breeze You Whisper: Poems* and *Calla & Édourd* (a novella) were published by Hidden Brook Press, Brighton (2011 and 2009, respectively). You can learn more and read her book reviews at https://kathrynmacdonald.com

Katie Thompson is from Vancouver Island and resides in Southwestern Ontario.

Ruth McKinney is a poet living in Kingston, Ontario. A poetry junkie, she has been writing—for love or money—all her life and is thrilled to finally be able to do it just for love.

Susan Alexander is grateful for Wintergreen, a thin place where poems seem to flourish along with leopard frogs, lightning bugs and little green snakes. She would like to thank Lorna, Rena and her crew, and all of the poets for so generously sharing words and silence.

Susan Wismer goes for long walks, writes poetry, walks some more. Within her family, which is broadly defined, she is famous for eclectic and occasionally unpalatable vegetarian cookery and for a quirked sense of humour, passed down from her mother. She lives on Anishinaabe territory at Georgian Bay, in Ontario.

Suzanne Doerge lives in Ottawa where she works with women across diversity for their voices to be heard. Her poetry has been published in Liaison and In/Words Magazine anthology, *Dis(s)ent*. Having fallen hopelessly in love with words, she was delighted to spend another week with this community of poets.

Wintergreen Studios Press is an independent literary press. It is affiliated with the not-for-profit educational retreat centre, Wintergreen Studios, and supports the work of Wintergreen Studios by publishing works related to education, the arts, and the environment.

www.wintergreenstudios.com

www.ingramcontent.com/pod-product-compliance
Lightning Source LLC
Chambersburg PA
CBHW070753050426
42449CB00010B/2459